HID IN MY HEART

The Word of God in Times of Need

Florence M. Taylor

Thy word have I hid in mine heart.
—Psalm 119:11

What are your spiritual needs? Courage? Faith? Hope? Love? Forgiveness? Wisdom? Peace? Joy? Inexhaustible treasures are waiting for you in the pages of God's word—treasures sufficient to meet every need of your life. This book presents passages from the King James Version to be "learned by heart" for ready recall in times of need.

The treasures of the Bible have the power to guide us and to enrich our lives. Above all, they strengthen us in time of temptation. When deeply cherished in our minds —hidden in our hearts—they stand ever ready to answer our deepest spiritual needs.

HID IN MY HEART

Hid in My Heart

THE WORD OF GOD IN TIMES OF NEED

by Florence M. Taylor

A CROSSROAD BOOK

THE SEABURY PRESS · NEW YORK

The Seabury Press
815 Second Avenue
New York, N.Y. 10017

Copyright © 1974 by Florence M. Taylor
Design by Paula Wiener
Printed in the United States of America

Library of Congress Cataloging in Publication Data

Bible. English. Authorized. Selections. 1974.
   Hid in my heart: the word of God in times of
need.

   "A Crossroad book."
   I. Taylor, Florence Marian Tompkins, 1892–
comp. II. Title.
BS391.2.T39   1974   220.5′203   74–9828
ISBN 0–8164–1186–7

Thy word have I hid in mine heart,
that I might not sin against thee.
> —Psalm 119:11

Evening, and morning, and at noon
will I pray, . . .
> —Psalm 55:17

Contents

NOON   45

To You—The Reader

This book contains chosen passages from the Bible to be "learned by heart" for ready recall in times of need. Its purpose is to entice you into an exploration of the treasures of the Bible; they have the power to guide you and to enrich your life.

O taste and see that the Lord is good.   —Psalm 34:8

Then, once having tasted, you can share Jeremiah's experience:

Thy words were found, and I did eat them; and thy word was unto me the joy and rejoicing of mine heart. . . .
                                                —Jeremiah 15:16

"To learn by heart"—what a lovely phrase! How much more satisfying than the matter-of-fact "to memorize"! How much nearer to the Biblical affirmation:

Thy word have I hid in mine heart.   —Psalm 119:11

Why learn God's words by heart? *Isn't it enough to have them readily available in the Bible—with a Concordance near at hand?*

A moment's thought should be enough to enable us to answer that question decisively in the negative. One reason for "hiding the Word in our hearts" is that we "may not sin" against God (cf. Psalm 119:11).

Temptations to sin usually strike us with complete unexpectedness. There isn't enough time to "search the Scriptures" (John 5:39) for guidance and strength. Consider the story of Jesus' temptation: Matthew 4:1–11; Luke 4:1–13.

How did Jesus meet every temptation put forth by Satan? By an apt quotation from the sacred writings. He did not need to consult a Concordance, nor to spend time in a lengthy examination of the precious scrolls. He simply dipped into the treasures that had been stored in his mind and heart since the days of his childhood; and he came up with the exact strengthening help that he needed.

So we too, following the example of our Lord and Saviour, need to cherish in our hearts the saving wisdom God has preserved for us through the centuries in his Holy Word.

Although the Word in our hearts can strengthen us to withstand temptation, that is by no means all it can do. What are your other spiritual needs? Courage? Faith? Hope? Love? Forgiveness? Wisdom? Peace? Joy? Inexhaustible treasures are waiting for you in the pages of God's Word —treasures sufficient to meet every need of your life.

God shall supply all your need according to his riches in glory by Christ Jesus.   —Philippians 4:19

Evening—Morning—Noon

Usually we think of the morning as the beginning, and evening as the end of the day. It is interesting, however, to discover that in the Creation story (Genesis 1 and 2) this taken-for-granted order is reversed:

And the evening and the morning were the first day.

—Genesis 1:5

The observance of the Jewish sabbath, the seventh day, follows this Biblical order: it starts with the going down of the sun on Friday, and ends with sundown on Saturday.

Another instance of this reversed order is found in one of the Psalms:

Evening, and morning, and at noon will I pray.

—Psalm 55:17

Is there some hidden wisdom and divine guidance to be found in this reversal of our usual thinking? Is there some spiritual blessing to be gained in thinking of the evening, not as an end, but as a new beginning? Carried to its logical conclusion, this insight also suggests that the evening time of life should be seen not as the end of life but as a time of preparation for life eternal.

The Biblical prayers and meditations in this book are gathered into three sections suggested by the verse above: Evening (with a section "Special Meditations for the Evening of Life"); Morning; Noon.

It is the prayer of the compiler that every reader of this book may find in its pages the satisfaction of deep spiritual needs, and may embark on an inner adventure of "hiding in his heart" the particular nuggets of truth and inspiration which speak to his specific needs.

FLORENCE M. TAYLOR

Columbus, Ohio
March, 1974

Evening

When we reverse the usual order, and try to recognize the evening as the beginning instead of as the end of the day, we become aware of a difference in the direction of our thinking. If we see the evening as the end of the day, our thoughts are still hopelessly entangled with the activities which have absorbed our attention and energies during the daylight hours. If we think of it as the beginning of the new day, our attention focuses not on past problems and difficulties but on new challenges and opportunities. In the one instance we are looking backward; and in the other we are looking forward. And this change in direction in itself may be a first step in preparation for a good night's sleep.

Sleep—what a miracle it is! And how we take for granted this mysterious gift of God! What happens when we sleep? Who can tell?

We know, when our bodies are exhausted, the blessedness

of complete relaxation that comes to us during the hours of unconsciousness. We know, because we have experienced it countless times, the renewal and restoration that restful sleep provides.

We know too the opposite experience of exhaustion that expresses itself in restless twisting and turning, the haunting anxieties and frustrations, the troubled dreams and imaginings that sometimes prevent the processes of restoration from fulfilling their blessed ministry.

Through both experiences we recognize that sleep is not only a great and beneficent mystery, but that it is an absolute necessity even for our continued existence. What we fail to recognize sometimes is that while our physical bodies are being renewed and revitalized, a parallel process is simultaneously renewing and revitalizing our spirits.

In Psalms we read:

He giveth his beloved sleep.   —Psalm 127:2

In the Revised Standard Version this verse reads:

He giveth his beloved in sleep.

Dr. Moffatt translates the same verse:

God's gifts come to his loved ones, as they sleep.

Whichever translation you prefer, the basic meaning remains unchanged. The testimony of many saints agrees that when they lay their burdens on the Lord in evening meditations, the answer to their need is given during the night hours; and the solution to the problem, the guidance

they seek, is in their minds when they wake in the morning.
They have found in their own experience the truth:

For God speaketh once, yea twice, yet man perceiveth it
not.
In a dream, in a vision of the night, when deep sleep
falleth upon men, in slumberings upon the bed;
Then he openeth the ears of men, and sealeth their in-
structions.   —Job 33:14–16

In anticipation of a good night's sleep, we go through
a ritual of preparation: we bathe, dress in loose clothing,
prepare our bed with clean linen and warm covers, adjust
the temperature, open the window for fresh air.

Surely the preparation of our hearts and spirits is far more
essential than these procedures for our physical comfort.
How should we make such preparation? Would the following procedures be helpful?

REACH OUT to God, with a recognition of his reality, of
his omnipresence, of his omnipotence, of his everlastingness,
of his love for us.

ACKNOWLEDGE thankfully the uncounted "benefits" with
which he has loaded us (Psalm 68:19).

CONFESS honestly specific sins committed, and failure to
fulfill specific responsibilities.

ACCEPT gratefully God's forgiveness.

RENEW sincerely our commitment to God's way for our
lives, and resolve to do better tomorrow with God's help.

OPEN our hearts joyously to God's "peace . . . which
passeth all understanding" (Philippians 4:7).

This, or some similar spiritual preparation for sleep, will enable God to heal and restore us during the night hours in preparation for the challenges and opportunities, the trials and testings, the triumphs and the failures of the daylight hours.

The prayers and meditations in this section are arranged in accordance with this suggested procedure.

1
Reach Out

Reach out to God, with a recognition of his reality, of his omnipresence, of his omnipotence, of his everlastingness, of his love for us.

Too often we come into God's presence with our minds focused on our own needs and problems. We are too ready to pour out words of complaint, or bewilderment, or of petition for real or fancied needs.

Someone has said: "For every one who comes into the presence of God saying, 'Speak, Lord, for thy servant heareth,' there are ten who come saying, 'Hear, Lord, for thy servant speaketh.'"

When this is true of us, we need to hear God's words to us:

Be still, and know that I am God.   —Psalm 46:10

The Lord is in his holy temple: let all the earth keep silence
before him.   —Habakkuk 2:20

In returning and rest shall ye be saved; in quietness and in
confidence shall be your strength. . . .
                                         —Isaiah 30:15

*And after a time of reverent silence, waiting on the Lord,
we may make these words our prayer:*

Abide with us: for it is toward evening, and the day is far
spent.   —Luke 24:29

God's Reality

*(Perhaps it should be noted that the Bible makes no at-
tempt to prove God's reality: it simply invites each seeker
to experience it.)*

For who is God save the Lord? or who is a rock save our
God?
  It is God that girdeth me with strength, and maketh my
way perfect.
  He maketh my feet like hinds' feet, and setteth me upon
my high places.   —Psalm 18:31–33

 Happy is he that hath . . . God . . . for his help, whose
hope is in the Lord his God:
  Which made heaven, and earth, the sea, and all that
therein is: which keepeth truth for ever:

Which executeth judgment for the oppressed: which giveth food to the hungry. The Lord looseth the prisoners.

The Lord openeth the eyes of the blind: the Lord raiseth them that are bowed down: the Lord loveth the righteous.

—Psalm 146:5–8

Thou art my God, and I will praise thee: thou art my God, I will exalt thee.   —Psalm 118:28

Blessed be the Lord God . . . who only doeth wondrous things.

And blessed be his glorious name for ever: and let the whole earth be filled with his glory; Amen, and Amen.

—Psalm 72:18–19

O Lord our Lord, how excellent is thy name in all the earth! . . .

When I consider thy heavens, the work of thy fingers, the moon and the stars, which thou hast ordained;

What is man, that thou art mindful of him? and the son of man, that thou visitest him?   —Psalm 8:1, 3–4

The Lord God is a sun and shield: the Lord will give grace and glory: no good thing will he withhold from them that walk uprightly.   —Psalm 84:11

. . . Stand still, and consider the wondrous works of God.

—Job 37:14

I will praise thee, O Lord my God, with all my heart: and I will glorify thy name for evermore.   —Psalm 86:12

All nations whom thou hast made shall come and worship before thee, O Lord, and shall glorify thy name.

For thou art great, and doest wondrous things: thou art God alone.   —Psalm 86:9–10

Amen: Blessing, and glory, and wisdom, and thanksgiving, and honour, and power, and might, be unto our God for ever and ever.   —Revelation 7:12

God's Omnipresence

Whither shall I go from thy spirit? or whither shall I flee from thy presence?

If I ascend up into heaven, thou art there: if I make my bed in hell, behold, thou art there.

If I take the wings of the morning, and dwell in the uttermost parts of the sea;

Even there shall thy hand lead me, and thy right hand shall hold me.

If I say, Surely the darkness shall cover me; even the night shall be light about me.

Yea, the darkness hideth not from thee; but the night shineth as the day: the darkness and the light are both alike to thee.   —Psalm 139:7–12

Will God in very deed dwell with men on the earth? behold, heaven and the heaven of heavens cannot contain thee!   —II Chronicles 6:18

There is . . . one God and Father of all, who is above all, and through all, and in you all.   —Ephesians 4:4–6

Know ye not that ye are the temple of God, and that the Spirit of God dwelleth in you?   —I Corinthians 3:16

God that made the world and all things therein, seeing that he is Lord of heaven and earth, dwelleth not in temples made with hands;

Neither is worshipped with men's hands, as though he needed any thing, seeing he giveth to all life, and breath, and all things;

And hath made of one blood all nations of men for to dwell on all the face of the earth, and hath determined the times before appointed, and the bounds of their habitation;

That they should seek the Lord, if haply they might feel after him, and find him, though he be not far from every one of us:

For in him we live, and move, and have our being . . . .
          —Acts 17:24–28

God's Omnipotence

Hast thou not known? hast thou not heard, that the ever-lasting God, the Lord, the Creator of the ends of the earth, fainteth not, neither is weary? there is no searching of his understanding.

He giveth power to the faint; and to them that have no might, he increaseth strength.   —Isaiah 40:28–29

Blessed be thou, Lord God . . . for ever and ever.

Thine, O Lord, is the greatness, and the power, and the glory, and the victory, and the majesty: for all that is in the heaven and in the earth is thine; thine is the kingdom, O Lord, and thou art exalted as head above all.

Both riches and honour come of thee, and thou reignest over all; and in thine hand is power and might; and in thine hand it is to make great, and to give strength unto all.

—I Chronicles 29:10–12

And I heard as it were the voice of a great multitude, and as the voice of many waters, and as the voice of mighty thunderings, saying, Alleluia: for the Lord God omnipotent reigneth. —Revelation 19:6

O come, let us sing unto the Lord: let us make a joyful noise to the rock of our salvation.

Let us come before his presence with thanksgiving, and make a joyful noise unto him with psalms.

For the Lord is a great God, and a great King above all gods.

In his hand are the deep places of the earth: the strength of the hills is his also.

The sea is his, and he made it: and his hands formed the dry land.

O come, let us worship and bow down: let us kneel before the Lord our maker.

For he is our God; and we are the people of his pasture, and the sheep of his hand. . . . —Psalm 95:1–7

Be thou exalted, Lord, in thine own strength: so will we sing and praise thy power. —Psalm 21:13

. . . Blessed be the name of God for ever and ever: for wisdom and might are his:

And he changeth the times and the seasons: he removeth

kings, and setteth up kings: he giveth wisdom unto the wise, and knowledge to them that know understanding.

He revealeth the deep and secret things: he knoweth what is in the darkness, and the light dwelleth with him.

—Daniel 2:20–22

God's Everlastingness

Lord, thou hast been our dwelling place in all generations.

Before the mountains were brought forth, or ever thou hadst formed the earth and the world, even from everlasting to everlasting, thou art God.   —Psalm 90:1–2

The glory of the Lord shall endure for ever: . . .

I will sing unto the Lord as long as I live: I will sing praise to my God while I have my being.

—Psalm 104:31, 33

Of old thou hast laid the foundation of the earth: and the heavens are the work of thy hands.

They shall perish, but thou shalt endure: yea, all of them shall wax old like a garment; as a vesture shalt thou change them, and they shall be changed:

But thou art the same, and thy years shall have no end.

—Psalm 102:25–27

They that trust in the Lord shall be as mount Zion, which cannot be removed, but abideth for ever.

As the mountains are round about Jerusalem, so the Lord is round about his people from henceforth even for ever.

—Psalm 125:1–2

All thy works shall praise thee, O Lord; and thy saints shall bless thee.

They shall speak of the glory of thy kingdom, and talk of thy power. . . .

Thy kingdom is an everlasting kingdom, and thy dominion endureth throughout all generations.

—Psalm 145:10–13

Thine is the kingdom, and the power, and the glory, for ever. Amen.   —Matthew 6:13

God's Love for Us

Who shall separate us from the love of Christ? shall tribulation, or distress, or persecution, or famine, or nakedness, or peril, or sword? . . .

Nay, in all these things we are more than conquerors through him that loved us.

For I am persuaded, that neither death, nor life, nor angels, nor principalities, nor powers, nor things present, nor things to come,

Nor height, nor depth, nor any other creature, shall be able to separate us from the love of God, which is in Christ Jesus our Lord.   —Romans 8:35–39

For God so loved the world, that he gave his only begotten Son, that whosoever believeth in him, should not perish, but have everlasting life.   —John 3:16

Ye are the sons of the living God.   —Hosea 1:10

Behold, what manner of love the Father hath bestowed
upon us, that we should be called the sons of God. . . .

—I John 3:1

In this was manifested the love of God toward us, because
that God sent his only begotten Son into the world, that we
might live through him.

Herein is love, not that we loved God, but that he loved
us, and sent his Son to be the propitiation for our sins.

—I John 4:9–10

2
Acknowledge

Acknowledge thankfully the uncounted "benefits" with which God has "loaded" us (Psalm 68:19).

Thankfulness is a rare quality of living. Too many of us reach out greedy hands for what seem to us the "good things" of life, and are never satisfied. Our "wants" are insatiable and our gratitude is far too rare.

Years ago I heard the late Dr. Truman B. Douglass preach a children's sermon on "Barnacles." He had some barnacles to show the children, and pointed out how hard and scratchy and dangerous they were for the unwary bather who happened to come up against them under the water.

He explained that very early in life the small barnacle attaches itself to the surface of a submerged boat, or a pier, or a sunken log—and never moves from that place again. Hidden in its shell, it lies in wait, and when some smaller bit of life swims by, it reaches out and grabs it, and con-

Jesus did not utter a word of condemnation. Neither does he condemn us. In this recall of the day's activities, it is our conscience that condemns us. As we form the habit of reviewing the events of the day in God's presence, he will be enabled to give us a conscience increasingly sensitive to his revelation and guidance.

The recognition and confession of our sins enables us to follow the exhortation of the writer of Hebrews:

Let us draw near with a true heart in full assurance of faith, having our hearts sprinkled from an evil conscience. . . .

—Hebrews 10:22

. . . Repent, and turn yourselves from all your transgressions; so iniquity shall not be your ruin.

Cast away from you all your transgressions, whereby ye have transgressed; and make you a new heart and a new spirit: for why will ye die, O house of Israel?

For I have no pleasure in the death of him that dieth, saith the Lord God: wherefore turn yourselves, and live ye.

—Ezekiel 18:30–32

Therefore also now, saith the Lord, turn ye even to me with all your heart, and with fasting, and with weeping, and with mourning:

And rend your heart, and not your garments, and turn unto the Lord your God: for he is gracious and merciful. . . .   —Joel 2:12–13

I know that in me (that is, in my flesh,) dwelleth no good thing: for to will is present with me; but how to perform that which is good I find not.

For the good that I would I do not: but the evil which I would not, that I do.   —Romans 7:18–19

With the heart man believeth unto righteousness; and with the mouth confession is made unto salvation.

—Romans 10:10

If we say that we have no sin, we deceive ourselves, and the truth is not in us.

If we confess our sins, he is faithful and just to forgive us our sins, and to cleanse us from all unrighteousness.

—I John 1:8–9

He that covereth his sins shall not prosper; but whoso confesseth and forsaketh them shall have mercy.

—Proverbs 28:13

Have mercy upon me, O God, according to thy lovingkindness: according unto the multitude of thy tender mercies blot out my transgressions.

Wash me thoroughly from mine iniquity, and cleanse me from my sin.

For I acknowledge my transgressions, and my sin is ever before me.   —Psalm 51:1–3

Create in me a clean heart, O God; and renew a right spirit within me.   —Psalm 51:10

4
Accept

Accept gratefully God's forgiveness.

In spite of the fact that God's promise of forgiveness to those who truly repent is repeated over and over in the pages of both the Old and the New Testaments, many repenetant sinners still carry an unnecessary burden of guilt.

It is not enough to read God's promise: it is necessary for each person to appropriate it, to take possession of it, and to know the joy of accepting it thankfully and starting out anew.

Peter, after his denial, accepted God's forgiveness and went on to a life of triumphant witnessing for his Lord. Judas, unable to accept it, killed himself.

Let the wicked forsake his way, and the unrighteous man his thoughts: and let him return unto the Lord, and he will have mercy upon him; and to our God, for he will abundantly pardon.

For my thoughts are not your thoughts, neither are your ways my ways, saith the Lord.

For as the heavens are higher than the earth, so are my ways higher than your ways, and my thoughts than your thoughts.   —Isaiah 55:7–9

Come now, and let us reason together, saith the Lord: though your sins be as scarlet, they shall be white as snow; though they be red like crimson, they shall be as wool.
—Isaiah 1:18

. . . Be of good cheer; thy sins be forgiven thee.
—Matthew 9:2

For as the heaven is high above the earth, so great is [God's] mercy toward them that fear him.

As far as the east is from the west, so far hath he removed our transgressions from us.

Like as a father pitieth his children, so the Lord pitieth them that fear him.

For he knoweth our frame; he remembereth that we are dust.   —Psalm 103:11–14

. . . unto thee, O Lord, do I lift up my soul.

For thou, Lord, art good, and ready to forgive; and plenteous in mercy unto all them that call upon thee.
—Psalm 86:4–5

To the Lord our God belong mercies and forgivenesses, though we have rebelled against him.   —Daniel 9:9

If thou, Lord, shouldest mark iniquities, O Lord, who shall stand?

But there is forgiveness with thee, . . .

—Psalm 130:3–4

Blessed is he whose transgression is forgiven, whose sin is covered.   —Psalm 32:1

5
Renew

Renew sincerely our commitment to God's way for our lives, and resolve to do better, with God's help.

The next step in preparation for God's ministry to us during the night's rest is the renewal of our commitment to him.

Having reached out to him in faith, having gratefully acknowledged his countless blessings, having confessed our sins and shortcomings, and accepted his assurance of forgiveness, we are ready once more to affirm his Lordship over our lives, and to renew our commitment to him and to his holy and eternal purpose for us.

Teach me, O Lord, the way of thy statutes; and I shall keep it unto the end.

Give me understanding, and I shall keep thy law; yea, I shall observe it with my whole heart.

Make me to go in the path of thy commandments; for
therein do I delight.   —Psalm 119:33–35

Search me, O God, and know my heart: try me, and know
my thoughts:
    And see if there be any wicked way in me, and lead me in
the way everlasting.   —Psalm 139:23–24

Teach me to do thy will; for thou art my God: thy spirit is
good; lead me into the land of uprightness.

                                          —Psalm 143:10

I beseech you therefore, brethren, by the mercies of God,
that ye present your bodies a living sacrifice, holy, acceptable
unto God, which is your reasonable service.
    And be not conformed to this world: but be ye trans-
formed by the renewing of your mind, that ye may prove
what is that good, and acceptable, and perfect, will of God.

                                          —Romans 12:1–2

Jesus said: Whosoever heareth these sayings of mine, and
doeth them, I will liken him unto a wise man, which built
his house upon a rock:
    And the rain descended, and the floods came, and the
winds blew, and beat upon that house; and it fell not: for it
was founded upon a rock.   —Matthew 7:24–25

6
Open Our Hearts

Open our hearts joyously to God's "peace which passeth all understanding."

If we have followed these steps in preparation for the restoration and renewal of our spirits during the night hours, God's peace will already have taken possession of our minds and hearts—and we are ready to say with the psalmist:

Into thine hand I commit my spirit, . . . O Lord God of truth.   —Psalm 31:5

Then we are ready to claim as our own the Bible promises:

Thou wilt keep him in perfect peace, whose mind is stayed on thee: because he trusteth in thee.   —Isaiah 26:3

When thou liest down, thou shalt not be afraid: yea, thou
shalt lie down, and thy sleep shall be sweet.

—Proverbs 3:24

I will both lay me down in peace, and sleep: for thou, Lord,
only makest me dwell in safety.   —Psalm 4:8

And the work of righteousness shall be peace; and the effect
of righteousness quietness and assurance for ever.

—Isaiah 32:17

Let the peace of God rule in your hearts.

—Colossians 3:15

The peace of God, which passeth all understanding, shall
keep your hearts and minds through Christ Jesus.

—Philippians 4:7

Jesus said: Peace I leave with you, my peace I give unto you:
not as the world giveth, give I unto you. Let not your heart
be troubled, neither let it be afraid.   —John 14:27

Special Meditations for the Evening of Life

Just as the evening of the day can be thought of as a beginning instead of as an end, so old age, the eventide of life, can be thought of, not as the ending of our lives, but as the beginning of eternal life. It can be understood as a time of preparation for the life to come.

Those of us who have lived to "a ripe old age" can look back to the time when death seemed a frightening, much-to-be-dreaded calamity—not so much for what it would mean to us, as for what it might mean to those near and dear to us for whose happiness and welfare we felt responsible. But as the years passed, our responsibilities decreased, until in time, we knew that for good or ill, our major work was done.

What a beneficent plan of God's to allow this time for the gradual loosening of the ties that bind us to this life, this time of decreasing physical activity, of narrowing circles of concern! How we should welcome the imposed in-

activity, and joyfully relax, taking advantage of the physi-
cally idle hours to give ourselves wholeheartedly to the
things of the spirit: to praise and thankfulness to the Father
God; to genuine repentance for past failures; to grateful ac-
ceptance of spiritual baptism and cleansing; to a readiness to
witness for our Lord and Saviour to anyone he sends us; to
a ministry of intercessory prayer; to a living testimony of
how God's goodness is sufficient for every need, physical,
mental and spiritual; to face death simply and undramat-
ically, keeping ourselves

in the love of God, looking for the mercy of our Lord Jesus
Christ unto eternal life.   —Jude, vs. 21

What treasures God has provided in his Word for us to
"hide in our hearts" for our spiritual nourishment during
the evening time of our lives!

O taste and see that the Lord is good. . . .
                                         —Psalm 34:8

Cast me not off in the time of old age; forsake me not when
my strength faileth. . . .
   O God, thou has taught me from my youth: and hitherto
have I declared thy wondrous works.
   Now also when I am old and greyheaded, O God, forsake
me not; until I have showed thy strength unto this genera-
tion, and thy power to everyone that is to come.
                                         —Psalm 71:9, 17–19

Jesus said: My sheep hear my voice, and I know them, and
they follow me:

And I give unto them eternal life; and they shall never perish, neither shall any man pluck them out of my hand.

My Father, which gave them me, is greater than all; and no man is able to pluck them out of my Father's hand.

I and my Father are one.   —John 10:27–30

. . . The gift of God is eternal life through Jesus Christ our Lord.   —Romans 6:23

But ye, beloved, building up yourselves on your most holy faith, praying in the Holy Ghost,

Keep yourselves in the love of God, looking for the mercy of our Lord Jesus Christ unto eternal life. . . .

Now unto him that is able to keep you from falling, and to present you faultless before the presence of his glory with exceeding joy,

To the only wise God our Saviour, be glory and majesty, dominion and power, both now and ever. Amen.

                —Jude, vss. 20–25

Jesus said: Verily, verily, I say unto you, He that heareth my word, and believeth on him that sent me, hath everlasting life, and shall not come into condemnation; but is passed from death unto life.   —John 5:24

This is the record, that God hath given to us eternal life, and this life is in his Son.

He that hath the Son hath life; and he that hath not the Son of God hath not life.

These things have I written unto you that believe on the name of the Son of God; that ye may know that ye have eternal life, and that ye may believe on the name of the Son of God.   —I John 5:11–13

Surely goodness and mercy shall follow me all the days of my life: and I will dwell in the house of the Lord for ever.
—Psalm 23:6

In the way of righteousness is life: and in the pathway thereof there is no death.   —Proverbs 12:28

If ye then be risen with Christ, seek those things which are above, where Christ sitteth on the right hand of God.

Set your affection on things above, not on things of the earth.

For ye are dead, and your life is hid with Christ in God.

When Christ, who is our life, shall appear, then shall ye also appear with him in glory.   —Colossians 3:1–4

None of us liveth to himself, and no man dieth to himself.

For whether we live, we live unto the Lord; and whether we die, we die unto the Lord: whether we live therefore, or die, we are the Lord's.   —Romans 14:7–8

I have fought a good fight, I have finished my course, I have kept the faith.   —II Timothy 4:7

Eye hath not seen, nor ear heard, neither have entered into the heart of man, the things which God hath prepared for them that love him.   —I Corinthians 2:9

Jesus said: Verily, verily, I say unto you, He that believeth on me hath everlasting life.   —John 6:47

For our light affliction, which is but for a moment, worketh for us a far more exceeding and eternal weight of glory;

While we look not at the things which are seen, but at

the things which are not seen: for the things which are seen are temporal; but the things which are not seen are eternal.

For we know that if our earthly house of this tabernacle were dissolved, we have a building of God, an house not made with hands, eternal in the heavens.

—II Corinthians 4:17–18; 5:1

Morning

The hours of the night are gone; morning has come. With the alarm clock's jarring noise, you open your eyes—and the duties and responsibilities of your life crowd in upon you. No time now for leisurely devotions (unless, indeed, you have set your alarm a bit early?); but always there is time for a quick lifting of your heart to God. This again is one of the times when the Word "hidden in your heart" is instantly available, and can set the tone for the entire day.

1
On Waking

Even while you are stretching your body and reluctantly preparing to lift yourself out of bed, you can focus your mind on one or more of these bits of spiritual inspiration:

This is the day which the Lord hath made; we will rejoice
and be glad in it.   —Psalm 118:24

Cause me to hear thy lovingkindness in the morning; for in
thee do I trust: cause me to know the way wherein I should
walk; for I lift up my soul unto thee.   —Psalm 143:8

O God, thou art my God; early will I seek thee: my soul
thirsteth for thee. . . .
    Because thy lovingkindness is better than life, my lips
shall praise thee.   —Psalm 63:1, 3

With my soul have I desired thee in the night; yea, with my
spirit within me will I seek thee early: for when thy judg-
ments are in the earth, the inhabitants of the world will
learn righteousness.   —Isaiah 26:9

What doth the Lord thy God require of thee, but to fear the
Lord thy God, to walk in all his ways, and to love him, and
to serve the Lord thy God with all thy heart and with all thy
soul?   —Deuteronomy 10:12

He hath showed thee, O man, what is good; and what doth
the Lord require of thee, but to do justly, and to love mercy,
and to walk humbly with thy God?   —Micah 6:8

And let the beauty of the Lord our God be upon us: and
establish thou the work of our hands upon us; yea, the work
of our hands establish thou it.   —Psalm 90:17

2
Praise the Lord!

You might start your day with singing! Every Christian family should be a singing family.

It is amazingly difficult to be irritable or fault-finding if it is necessary to interrupt the Doxology in order to make a critical comment or to correct some misbehavior!

Had you ever realized how much the Bible has to say about singing? Here are a few verses to remember:

Let the saints be joyful in glory: let them sing aloud upon their beds.   —Psalm 149:5

O sing unto the Lord a new song; for he hath done marvellous things. . . .   —Psalm 98:1

Sing unto the Lord, O ye saints of his, and give thanks at the remembrance of his holiness.   —Psalm 30:4

I will sing unto the Lord as long as I live: I will sing praise
to my God while I have my being.   —Psalm 104:33

Praise ye the Lord. . . .
  From the rising of the sun unto the going down of the
same the Lord's name is to be praised.
                                          —Psalm 113:1, 3

Praise ye the Lord. Praise God in his sanctuary: praise him
in the firmament of his power.
  Praise him for his mighty acts: praise him according to
his excellent greatness.
  Praise him with the sound of the trumpet: praise him
with the psaltery and harp.
  Praise him with the timbrel and dance: praise him with
stringed instruments and organs.
  Praise him upon the loud cymbals: praise him upon the
high sounding cymbals.
  Let every thing that hath breath praise the Lord. Praise
ye the Lord.   —Psalm 150

. . . Be filled with the Spirit . . . making melody in your
heart to the Lord.   —Ephesians 5:18–19

3
While Dressing

*What better thing to call to mind while you are dressing
than these words of Jesus?*

And why take ye thought for raiment? Consider the lilies of
the field, how they grow; they toil not, neither do they spin:

And yet I say unto you, That even Solomon in all his
glory was not arrayed like one of these.

Wherefore, if God so clothe the grass of the field, which
today is, and tomorrow is cast into the oven, shall he not
much more clothe you, O ye of little faith?

Therefore take no thought, saying, What shall we eat? or,
What shall we drink? or, Wherewithal shall we be clothed?
. . . for your heavenly Father knoweth that ye have need
of all these things.

But seek ye first the kingdom of God, and his righteousness; and all these things shall be added unto you.

—Matthew 6:28–33

Godliness with contentment is great gain. For we brought nothing into this world, and it is certain we can carry nothing out.

And having food and raiment, let us be therewith content.   —I Timothy 6:6–8

4
At Breakfast

The first meal of the day might well be an occasion of gratitude to God for his provision for all our needs—not just for food for our bodies, but also for spiritual nourishment. This is a good time to remember:

God shall supply all your need, according to his riches in glory by Christ Jesus.   —Philippians 4:19

Man shall not live by bread alone, but by every word of God.   —Luke 4:4

Jesus said unto them, I am the bread of life: he that cometh to me shall never hunger; and he that believeth on me shall never thirst.   —John 6:35

Verily, verily, I say unto you, he that believeth on me hath everlasting life.

I am that bread of life.

Your fathers did eat manna in the wilderness, and are dead.

This is the bread which cometh down from heaven, that a man may eat thereof, and not die.

I am the living bread which came down from heaven: if any man eat of this bread, he shall live for ever.

—John 6:47–51

Noon

"Noon" covers more than the stroke of twelve at midday. "Evening—morning—noon" suggests that "noontide" covers all that occurs between morning and evening.

This is the period of our greatest activity. This is the part of the day when

Man goeth forth unto his work and to his labour until the evening. —Psalm 104:23

This is the part of the day when many of us leave the comfort and security of our homes to expose ourselves to the confusion, the competition, the frustrations and annoyances of the office, the factory, the laboratory, the school, the foundry, the hospital, the market place, and the thousand and one other places where people carry on the necessary labor for the functioning of the life of the community.

"Noon" carries with it the suggestion of heat—the "heat of the battle" perhaps?

This is the part of the day when the pace speeds up, when the pressure increases, when there is little time for thoughtful decisions, when physical weariness and anxieties weaken our spiritual defenses, when our resistance is lowered, and temptations to irritability and discouragement, to selfish absorption in our own concerns and lack of concern for others, to indifference and irresponsibility beset us on every side.

This is a time when the Word "hid in our hearts" can reinforce the holy commitments and resolves made in quiet hours; when we can draw strength and courage from deep within; when the remembrance of God's faithful promises can enable us to stand fast, and to live triumphantly.

When You Are about to Be Married

And the Lord God said, It is not good that the man should be alone; I will make him an help meet for him. . . .

And the Lord God . . . made he a woman, and brought her unto the man.

And Adam said, This is now bone of my bones, and flesh of my flesh: she shall be called Woman, because she was taken out of Man.

Therefore shall a man leave his father and his mother, and shall cleave unto his wife: and they shall be one flesh.

—Genesis 2:18, 21–24

Let the husband render unto the wife due benevolence: and likewise also the wife unto the husband.

—I Corinthians 7:3

Live joyfully with the wife whom thou lovest.

—Ecclesiastes 9:9

Blessed is every one that feareth the Lord; that walketh in his ways.

For thou shalt eat the labour of thine hands: happy shalt thou be, and it shall be well with thee.

Thy wife shall be as a fruitful vine by the sides of thine house: thy children like olive plants round about thy table.

Behold, that thus shall the man be blessed that feareth the Lord. . . .

Yea, thou shalt see thy children's children. . . .

—Psalm 128:1–4, 6

Jesus said: Have ye not read, that he which made them at the beginning made them male and female,

And said, For this cause shall a man leave father and mother, and shall cleave to his wife: and they twain shall be one flesh?

Wherefore they are no more twain, but one flesh. What therefore God hath joined together, let not man put asunder.   —Matthew 19:4–6

Love (charity) suffereth long, and is kind; love envieth not; love vaunteth not itself, is not puffed up,

Doth not behave itself unseemly, seeketh not her own, is not easily provoked, thinketh no evil;

Rejoiceth not in iniquity, but rejoiceth in the truth;

Beareth all things, believeth all things, hopeth all things, endureth all things.

Love never faileth.   —I Corinthians 13:4–8

Who can find a virtuous woman? for her price is far above rubies.

The heart of her husband doth safely trust in her. . . .

She will do him good and not evil all the days of her life. . . .

She openeth her mouth with wisdom; and in her tongue is the law of kindness. . . .

Her children arise up, and call her blessed; her husband also, and he praiseth her.

—Proverbs 31:10–12, 26, 28

When You Are about to Become a Parent

Lo, children are an heritage of the Lord. . . .

—Psalm 127:3

Hear, O Israel: the Lord our God is one Lord:
And thou shalt love the Lord thy God with all thine
heart, and with all thy soul, and with all thy might.
And these words, which I command thee this day, shall
be in thine heart:
And thou shalt teach them diligently unto thy children,
and shalt talk of them when thou sittest in thine house, and
when thou walkest by the way, and when thou liest down,
and when thou risest up.   —Deuteronomy 6:4–7

The father to the children shall make known thy truth.

—Isaiah 38:19

Ye fathers, provoke not your children to wrath: but bring them up in the nurture and admonition of the Lord.

—Ephesians 6:4

Train up a child in the way he should go; and when he is old, he will not depart from it.   —Proverbs 22:6

Like as a father pitieth his children, so the Lord pitieth them that fear him.

For he knoweth our frame; he remembereth that we are dust. . . .

. . . The mercy of the Lord is from everlasting to everlasting upon them that fear him, and his righteousness unto children's children.   —Psalm 103:13–14, 17

When You Are Afraid

The eternal God is thy refuge, and underneath are the everlasting arms. . . .   —Deuteronomy 33:27

Have not I commanded thee? Be strong and of a good courage; be not afraid, neither be thou dismayed: for the Lord
thy God is with thee whithersoever thou goest.
                                          —Joshua 1:9

Wait on the Lord: be of good courage, and he shall
strengthen thine heart: wait, I say, on the Lord.
                                          —Psalm 27:14

The Lord is my light and my salvation; whom shall I fear?
the Lord is the strength of my life; of whom shall I be
afraid?   —Psalm 27:1

God is our refuge and strength, a very present help in trouble.

Therefore will not we fear, though the earth be removed, and though the mountains be carried into the midst of the sea;

Though the waters thereof roar and be troubled, though the mountains shake with the swelling thereof. . . .

The Lord of hosts is with us; the God of Jacob is our refuge.   —Psalm 46:1–3, 7

The wicked flee when no man pursueth; but the righteous are bold as a lion.   —Proverbs 28:1

. . . O thou most High, what time I am afraid, I will trust in thee.   —Psalm 56:2–3

Behold, God is my salvation; I will trust, and not be afraid: for the Lord Jehovah is my strength and my song; he also is become my salvation.   —Isaiah 12:2

Fear not: for I have redeemed thee, I have called thee by thy name; thou art mine.

When thou passest through the waters, I will be with thee; and through the rivers, they shall not overflow thee: when thou walkest through the fire, thou shalt not be burned; neither shall the flame kindle upon thee.

For I am the Lord thy God, the Holy One of Israel, thy Saviour.   —Isaiah 43:1–3

In God have I put my trust: I will not be afraid what man can do unto me.   —Psalm 56:11

Jesus said: The cup which my Father hath given me, shall I not drink it?   —John 18:11

When You Are Angry

A soft answer turneth away wrath: but grievous words stir
up anger.   —Proverbs 15:1

He that is slow to anger is better than the mighty; and he
that ruleth his spirit than he that taketh a city.
                                            —Proverbs 16:32

An angry man stirreth up strife, and a furious man abound-
eth in transgression.   —Proverbs 29:22

Surely the churning of milk bringeth forth butter, and the
wringing of the nose bringeth forth blood: so the forcing of
wrath bringeth forth strife.   —Proverbs 30:33

A wrathful man stirreth up strife: but he that is slow to
anger appeaseth strife.   —Proverbs 15:18

not the sun go down upon your wrath.
—Ephesians 4:26

ll bitterness, and wrath, and anger, and clamour, and
eaking be put away from you, with all malice:
1 be ye kind one to another, tenderhearted, forgiving
other, even as God for Christ's sake has forgiven you.
—Ephesians 4:31–32

When You Are Carrying a Weight of Guilt

I say unto you, that likewise joy shall be in heaven over one sinner that repenteth, more than over ninety and nine just persons, which need no repentance.   —Luke 15:7

And Jesus said . . . , They that are whole need not a physician; but they that are sick.
    I came not to call the righteous, but sinners to repentance.   —Luke 5:31–32

Jesus said: Be of good cheer; thy sins be forgiven thee.
                              —Matthew 9:2

This is a faithful saying, and worthy of all acceptation, that Christ Jesus came into the world to save sinners.
                              —I Timothy 1:15

Seek ye the Lord while he may be found, call ye upon him while he is near:

Let the wicked forsake his way, and the unrighteous man his thoughts: and let him return unto the Lord, and he will have mercy upon him; and to our God, for he will abundantly pardon.   —Isaiah 55:6–7

The Lord is nigh unto them that are of a broken heart; and saveth such as be of a contrite spirit.   —Psalm 34:18

He hath not dealt with us after our sins; nor rewarded us according to our iniquities.

For as the heaven is high above the earth, so great is his mercy toward them that fear him.

As far as the east is from the west, so far hath he removed our transgressions from us.

Like as a father pitieth his children, so the Lord pitieth them that fear him.

For he knoweth our frame; he remembereth that we are dust.   —Psalm 103:10–14

When You Are Depressed and Unhappy

Whatsoever things are true, whatsoever things are honest, whatsoever things are just, whatsoever things are pure, whatsoever things are lovely, whatsoever things are of good report; if there be any virtue, and if there by any praise, think on these things. —Philippians 4:8

I sought the Lord, and he heard me, and delivered me from all my fears. —Psalm 34:4

The righteous cry, and the Lord heareth, and delivereth them out of all their troubles.
 The Lord is nigh unto them that are of a broken heart; and saveth such as be of a contrite spirit.
—Psalm 34:17–18

And Jesus said unto them, Why are ye so fearful? how is it that ye have no faith? —Mark 4:40

My soul melteth for heaviness: strengthen thou me according unto thy word.   —Psalm 119:28

Sing unto the Lord, O ye saints of his, and give thanks at
the remembrance of his holiness.
   . . . weeping may endure for a night, but joy cometh in
the morning.   —Psalm 30:4–5

The Lord healeth the broken in heart, and bindeth up their
wounds.   —Psalm 147:3

When You Are Enduring Physical Pain

If the Spirit of him that raised up Jesus from the dead dwell in you, he that raised up Christ from the dead shall also quicken your mortal bodies by his Spirit that dwelleth in you. . . .

The Spirit itself beareth witness with our spirit, that we are the children of God:

And if children, then heirs; heirs of God, and joint-heirs with Christ; if so be that we suffer with him, that we may be also glorified together.

For I reckon that the sufferings of this present time are not worthy to be compared with the glory which shall be revealed in us.

For the earnest expectation of the creature waiteth for the manifestation of the sons of God.

—Romans 8:11, 16–19

We desire that ye might be filled with the knowledge of God's will in all wisdom and spiritual understanding; . . .

Strengthened with all might, according to his glorious power, unto all patience and longsuffering with joyfulness;

Giving thanks unto the Father, which hath made us meet to be partakers of the inheritance of the saints in light:

Who hath delivered us from the power of darkness, and hath translated us into the kingdom of his dear Son.

—Colossians 1:9–13

Beloved, think it not strange concerning the fiery trial which is to try you, as though some strange thing happened unto you:

But rejoice, inasmuch as you are partakers of Christ's sufferings; that, when his glory shall be revealed, ye may be glad also with exceeding joy.   —I Peter 4:12–13

The God of all grace, who hath called us into his eternal glory by Christ Jesus, after that ye have suffered a while, make you perfect, stablish, strengthen, settle you.

To him be glory and dominion for ever and ever. Amen.

—I Peter 5:10–11

When You Are Facing a Difficult Situation That Seems to Have No Solution

The Lord thy God in the midst of thee is mighty; he will save, and he will rejoice over thee with joy; he will rest in his love, he will joy over thee with singing.
—Zephaniah 3:17

This is the word of the Lord . . . Not by might, nor by power, but by my spirit, saith the Lord of hosts.
—Zechariah 4:6

The Lord God is my strength, and he will make my feet like hinds' feet, and he will make me to walk upon my high places. —Habakkuk 3:19

(*Esther, a Jewish girl, married to King Ahasuerus, had been urged by her uncle, Mordecai, to plead with the king to spare the lives of the Jews who were threatened with extinction. Esther had objected that anyone who approached*

*the king without being summoned was in danger of instant
death. But Mordecai still insisted that she take the risk. He
said to her:)*

Who knoweth whether thou art come to the kingdom for
such a time as this?   —Esther 4:14

Teach me thy way, O Lord, and lead me in a plain
path. . . .   —Psalm 27:11

Thy word is a lamp unto my feet, and a light unto my path.
                                                  —Psalm 119:105

O send out thy light and thy truth: let them lead me; . . .
                                                  —Psalm 43:3

When You Are Facing the Death of a Loved One—or Your Own Imminent Death

Jesus said: Let not your heart be troubled: ye believe in God, believe also in me.

In my Father's house are many mansions: if it were not so, I would have told you. I go to prepare a place for you.

And if I go and prepare a place for you, I will come again, and receive you unto myself; that where I am, there ye may be also. —John 14:1–3

Art thou not from everlasting, O Lord my God, mine Holy One? we shall not die. —Habakkuk 1:12

For whether we live, we live unto the Lord; and whether we die, we die unto the Lord: whether we live therefore, or die, we are the Lord's.

For to this end Christ both died, and rose, and revived, that he might be Lord both of the dead and living.

—Romans 14:8–9

For if the dead rise not, then is not Christ raised:

And if Christ be not raised, your faith is vain; ye are yet in your sins.

Then they also which are fallen asleep in Christ are perished.

If in this life only we have hope in Christ, we are of all men most miserable.

But now is Christ risen from the dead, and become the first-fruits of them that slept.

—I Corinthians 15:16–20

But some man will say, How are the dead raised up? and with what body do they come?

Thou fool, that which thou sowest is not quickened, except it die:

And that which thou sowest, thou sowest not that body that shall be, but bare grain, it may chance of wheat, or of some other grain:

But God giveth it a body as it hath pleased him, and to every seed his own body. . . .

There is one glory of the sun, and another glory of the moon, and another glory of the stars: for one star differeth from another star in glory.

So also is the resurrection of the dead. It is sown in corruption; it is raised in incorruption:

It is sown in dishonour; it is raised in glory: it is sown in weakness; it is raised in power.

It is sown a natural body; it is raised a spiritual body.

—I Corinthians 15:35–44

For this corruptible must put on incorruption, and this mortal must put on immortality.

So when this corruptible shall have put on incorruption,

and this mortal shall have put on immortality, then shall
be brought to pass the saying that is written, Death is swal-
lowed up in victory.

O death, where is thy sting? O grave, where is thy victory? . . .

Thanks be to God, which giveth us the victory through
our Lord Jesus Christ.   —I Corinthians 15:53–57

And I heard a great voice out of heaven, saying, Behold, the
tabernacle of God is with men, and he will dwell with them,
and they shall be his people, and God himself shall be with
them, and be their God.

And God shall wipe away all tears from their eyes; and
there shall be no more death, neither sorrow, nor crying,
neither shall there be any more pain: for the former things
are passed away. . . . Behold, I make all things new.

—Revelation 21:3–5

When You Are Feeling That the Battle of Life Is Going against You

Be strong in the Lord, and in the power of his might.

Put on the whole armour of God, that ye may be able to stand against the wiles of the devil.

For we wrestle not against flesh and blood, but against principalities, against powers, against the rulers of the darkness of this world, against spiritual wickedness in high places.

Wherefore take unto you the whole armour of God, that ye may be able to withstand in the evil day, and having done all, to stand.

Stand therefore, having your loins girt about with truth, and having on the breastplate of righteousness;

And your feet shod with the preparation of the gospel of peace;

Above all, taking the shield of faith, wherewith ye shall be able to quench all the fiery darts of the wicked.

And take the helmet of salvation, and the sword of the Spirit, which is the word of God.

—Ephesians 6:10–17

God, who commanded the light to shine out of darkness, hath shined in our hearts, to give the light of the knowledge of the glory of God in the face of Jesus Christ. . . .

We are troubled on every side, yet not distressed; we are perplexed, but not in despair;

Persecuted, but not forsaken; cast down, but not destroyed;

Always bearing about in the body the dying of the Lord Jesus, that the life also of Jesus might be made manifest in our body.   —II Corinthians 4:6–10

When You Are Going on a Journey

Behold, I am with thee, and will keep thee in all places
whither thou goest.   —Genesis 28:15

If I take the wings of the morning, and dwell in the uttermost parts of the sea;
    Even there shall thy hand lead me, and thy right hand
shall hold me.   —Psalm 139:9–10

And the Lord said: My presence shall go with thee, and I
will give thee rest.   —Exodus 33:14

Be strong and of a good courage, fear not, nor be afraid . . .
for the Lord thy God, he it is that doth go with thee: he
will not fail thee, nor forsake thee.

                              —Deuteronomy 31:6

When You Are Lonely

. . . leave me not, neither forsake me, O God of my salvation.

When my father and my mother forsake me, then the Lord will take me up.   —Psalm 27:9–10

. . . they that know thy name will put their trust in thee: for thou, Lord, hast not forsaken them that seek thee.
                                                        —Psalm 9:10

The Lord is nigh unto all them that call upon him, to all that call upon him in truth.   —Psalm 145:18

God that made the world and all things therein . . . giveth to all life and breath, and all things: . . .

That they should seek the Lord, if haply they might feel after him and find him, though he be not far from every one of us:

For in him we live and move and have our being. . . .
                                                        —Acts 17:24–28

When You Are Moving into a New Home

Except the Lord build the house, they labour in vain that build it. . . . —Psalm 127:1

As for me and my house, we will serve the Lord.
—Joshua 24:15

And thou shalt rejoice in every good thing which the Lord thy God hath given unto thee, and unto thine house.
—Deuteronomy 26:11

For the mountains shall depart, and the hills be removed; but my kindness shall not depart from thee, neither shall the covenant of my peace be removed, saith the Lord that hath mercy on thee. . . .

And all thy children shall be taught of the Lord; and great shall be the peace of thy children.

In righteousness shalt thou be established. . . .
—Isaiah 54:10, 13–14

When You Are Searching for God

Oh that I knew where I might find him! . . .

Behold, I go forward, but he is not there; and backward, but I cannot perceive him;

On the left hand, where he doth work, but I cannot behold him: he hideth himself on the right hand, that I cannot see him:

But he knoweth the way that I take: when he hath tried me, I shall come forth as gold. —Job 23:3, 8-10

When thou saidst, Seek ye my face; my heart said unto thee, Thy face, Lord, will I seek. —Psalm 27:8

Turn ye unto me, saith the Lord of hosts, and I will turn unto you, saith the Lord of hosts. —Zechariah 1:3

Draw nigh to God, and he will draw nigh to you.
—James 4:8

God is a Spirit: and they that worship him must worship
him in spirit and in truth.   —John 4:24

The Lord is good unto them that wait for him, to the soul
that seeketh him.
   It is good that a man should both hope and quietly wait
for the salvation of the Lord.
                              —Lamentations 3:25–26

Seek the Lord, and ye shall live. . . .
   Seek him that made the seven stars and Orion, and turneth the shadow of death into the morning, and maketh the
day dark with night: that calleth for the waters of the sea,
and poureth them out upon the face of the earth: the Lord
is his name.   —Amos 5:6, 8

And ye shall seek me, and find me, when ye shall search for
me with all your heart.
   And I will be found of you, saith the Lord.
                              —Jeremiah 29:13–14

When You Are Starting a New Job

And whatsoever ye do, do it heartily, as to the Lord, and not unto men:
Knowing that of the Lord ye shall receive the reward of the inheritance: for ye serve the Lord Christ.

—Colossians 3:23–24

The labour of the righteous tendeth to life.

—Proverbs 10:16

Remember the sabbath day, to keep it holy.
Six days shalt thou labour, and do all thy work:
But the seventh day is the sabbath of the Lord thy God: in it thou shalt not do any work.   —Exodus 20:8–10

We are labourers together with God.

—I Corinthians 3:9

When You Are Tempted

There hath no temptation taken you but such as is common to man: but God is faithful, who will not suffer you to be tempted above that ye are able; but will with the temptation also make a way to escape, that ye may be able to bear it.

—I Corinthians 10:13

Blessed be the God and Father of our Lord Jesus Christ, which according to his abundant mercy hath begotten us again unto a lively hope by the resurrection of Jesus Christ from the dead,

To an inheritance incorruptible, and undefiled, and that fadeth not away, reserved in heaven for you,

Who are kept by the power of God through faith unto salvation ready to be revealed in the last time.

Wherein ye greatly rejoice, though now for a season, if need be, ye are in heaviness through manifold temptations:

That the trial of your faith, being much more precious

than of gold that perisheth, though it be tried with fire, might be found unto praise and honour and glory at the appearing of Jesus Christ:

Whom having not seen, ye love; in whom, though now ye see him not, yet believing, ye rejoice with joy unspeakable and full of glory.   —I Peter 1:3–8

Ye shall be holy unto me: for I the Lord am holy, and have severed you from other people, that ye should be mine.
                                        —Leviticus 20:26

When You Are Tempted by Pride

It is not good to eat much honey: so for men to search their own glory is not glory. —Proverbs 25:27

Let another man praise thee, and not thine own mouth, a stranger, and not thine own lips. —Proverbs 27:2

Pride goeth before destruction, and an haughty spirit before a fall.
    Better it is to be of an humble spirit with the lowly, than to divide the spoil with the proud.
—Proverbs 16:18–19

A man's pride shall bring him low: but honour shall uphold the humble in spirit. —Proverbs 29:23

Hear ye, and give ear; be not proud: for the Lord hath spoken. —Jeremiah 13:15

The pride of thine heart hath deceived thee, thou that dwellest in the clefts of the rock, whose habitation is high; that saith in his heart, Who shall bring me down to the ground?

Though thou exalt thyself as the eagle, and though thou set thy nest among the stars, thence will I bring thee down, saith the Lord.　　　　　　　　　　　—Obadiah, vss. 3–4

For all that is in the world, the lust of the flesh, and the lust of the eyes, and the pride of life, is not of the Father, but is of the world.

And the world passeth away, and the lust thereof: but he that doeth the will of God abideth for ever.

　　　　　　　　　　　　　　　—I John 2:15–17

[God speaks to Job] Hast thou an arm like God? or canst thou thunder with a voice like him?

Deck thyself now with majesty and excellency, and array thyself with glory and beauty.

Cast abroad the rage of thy wrath: and behold everyone that is proud, and abase him.

Look on everyone that is proud, and bring him low. . . .

Then will I also confess unto thee that thine own right hand can save thee.　　　　　　　　—Job 40:9–12, 14

The Lord doth hate . . . a proud look.

　　　　　　　　　　　　　　—Proverbs 6:16–17

Every one that is proud in heart is an abomination to the Lord.　　　　　　　　　　　　—Proverbs 16:5

An high look, and a proud heart . . . is sin.

　　　　　　　　　　　　　　—Proverbs 21:4

He that is of a proud heart stirreth up strife.

—Proverbs 28:25

Enter into the rock, and hide thee in the dust, for fear of the Lord, and for the glory of his majesty.

The lofty looks of man shall be humbled, and the haughtiness of men shall be bowed down, and the Lord alone shall be exalted in that day.

For the day of the Lord of hosts shall be upon every one that is proud and lofty, and upon every one that is lifted up; and he shall be brought low. . . .

And the loftiness of man shall be bowed down, and the haughtiness of men shall be made low: and the Lord alone shall be exalted in that day.   —Isaiah 2:10–12, 17

Jesus said: Whosoever exalteth himself shall be abased; and he that humbleth himself shall be exalted.

—Luke 14:11

Lord, thou hast heard the desire of the humble: thou wilt prepare their heart, thou wilt cause thine ear to hear.

—Psalm 10:17

For thus saith the high and lofty One that inhabiteth eternity, whose name is Holy; I dwell in the high and holy place with him also that is of a contrite and humble spirit, to revive the spirit of the humble, and to revive the heart of the contrite ones.   —Isaiah 57:15

Jesus called a little child unto him, and set him in the midst of them,

And said, Verily, I say unto you, Except ye be converted,

and become as little children, ye shall not enter into the kingdom of heaven.   —Matthew 18:2–3

Jesus said: Whosoever shall exalt himself shall be abased; and he that shall humble himself shall be exalted.
                                                    —Matthew 23:12

Yea, all of you be subject one to another, and be clothed with humility: for God resisteth the proud, and giveth grace to the humble.
   Humble yourselves therefore under the mighty hand of God, that he may exalt you in due time.
                                                    —I Peter 5:5–6

When You Are Tempted to Be Sorry for Yourself

Bless the Lord, O my soul: and all that is within me, bless his holy name.

Bless the Lord, O my soul, and forget not all his benefits:

Who forgiveth all thine iniquities; who healeth all thy diseases;

Who redeemeth thy life from destruction; who crowneth thee with lovingkindness and tender mercies;

Who satisfieth thy mouth with good things; so that thy youth is renewed like the eagle's.   —Psalm 103:1–5

How precious also are thy thoughts unto me, O God! how great is the sum of them!

If I should count them they are more in number than the sand. . . .   —Psalm 139:17–18

What shall I render unto the Lord for all his benefits toward me?

I will take the cup of salvation, and call upon the name of the Lord.   —Psalm 116:12–13

When You Are Tempted to Close Your Mind and Heart against the Needs of Your Neighbors

Whoso hath this world's good, and seeth his brother have need, and shutteth up his bowels of compassion from him, how dwelleth the love of God in him?

My little children, let us not love in word, neither in tongue; but in deed and in truth.   —I John 3:17–18

As every man hath received the gift, even so minister the same one to another, as good stewards of the manifold grace of God.   —I Peter 4:10

If ye fulfill the royal law according to the scripture, Thou shalt love thy neighbour as thyself, ye do well.

—James 2:8

Then shall the King say unto them on his right hand, Come, ye blessed of my Father, inherit the kingdom prepared for you from the foundation of the world:

For I was an hungered, and ye gave me meat: I was thirsty, and ye gave me drink: I was a stranger, and ye took me in:

Naked, and ye clothed me: I was sick, and ye visited me: I was in prison, and ye came unto me. . . .

Inasmuch as ye have done it unto one of the least of these my brethren, ye have done it unto me.

—Matthew 25:34–36, 40

Blessed be God, even the Father of our Lord Jesus Christ, the Father of mercies, and the God of all comfort;

Who comforteth us in all our tribulation, that we may be able to comfort them which are in any trouble, by the comfort wherewith we ourselves are comforted of God.

—II Corinthians 1:3–4

When You Are Tempted to Gossip

The words of a talebearer are as wounds.

—Proverbs 18:8

Thou shalt not bear false witness against thy neighbour.

—Exodus 20:16

Where no wood is, there the fire goeth out: so where there is no talebearer, the strife ceaseth.   —Proverbs 26:20

. . . the words of his mouth were smoother than butter, but war was in his heart: his words were softer than oil, yet were they drawn swords.   —Psalm 55:21

When You Are Tempted to Lie

Lord, who shall abide in thy tabernacle? who shall dwell in thy holy hill?

He that walketh uprightly, and worketh righteousness, and speaketh the truth in his heart.　　　　—Psalm 15:1–2

Teach me thy way, O Lord; I will walk in thy truth. . . .
　　　　　　　　　　　　　　　　　　—Psalm 86:11

I have chosen the way of truth: . . .
　　　　　　　　　　　　　　　　　　—Psalm 119:30

Let not mercy and truth forsake thee: bind them about thy neck; write them upon the table of thine heart.
　　　　　　　　　　　　　　　　　　—Proverbs 3:3

Ascribe ye greatness unto our God.

He is the Rock, his work is perfect: for all his ways are

judgment: a God of truth and without iniquity, just and
right is he.   —Deuteronomy 32:3–4

These are the things that ye shall do; Speak ye every man
the truth to his neighbour; execute the judgment of truth
and peace in your gates:
    And let none of you imagine evil in your hearts against
his neighbour; and love no false oath: for all these are things
that I hate, saith the Lord.   —Zechariah 8:16–17

Wherefore putting away lying, speak every man truth with
his neighbour: for we are members one of another.
                                            —Ephesians 4:25

Set a watch, O Lord, before my mouth; keep the door of my
lips.   —Psalm 141:3

When You Are Trying to Help Someone in Deep Trouble

Let us come boldly unto the throne of grace, that we may obtain mercy, and find grace to help in time of need.
—Hebrews 4:16

As in water face answereth to face, so the heart of man to man.
—Proverbs 27:19

Bear ye one another's burdens, and so fulfill the law of Christ.
—Galatians 6:2

We then that are strong ought to bear the infirmities of the weak, and not to please ourselves.
Let every one of us please his neighbour for his good to edification.
—Romans 15:1–2

But now hath God set the members every one of them in the body, as it hath pleased him. . . .

And whether one member suffer, all the members suffer with it; or one member be honored, all the members rejoice with it.

Now ye are the body of Christ, and members in particular.   —I Corinthians 12:18, 26–27

When You Are Walking through the Shadows

Though I walk through the valley of the shadow of death I will fear no evil; for thou art with me.   —Psalm 23:4

The Lord is good, a strong hold in the day of trouble; and he knoweth them that trust in him.   —Nahum 1:7

. . . weeping may endure for a night, but joy cometh in the morning.   —Psalm 30:5

In the world ye shall have tribulation: but be of good cheer; I have overcome the world.   —John 16:33

The people that walked in darkness have seen a great light; they that dwell in the land of the shadow of death, upon them hath the light shined.   —Isaiah 9:2

Seek him that maketh the seven stars and Orion, and turn-

eth the shadow of death into the morning. . . . the Lord
is his name.   —Amos 5:8

. . . The dayspring from on high hath visited us,
   To give light to them that sit in darkness and in the
shadow of death, to guide our feet into the way of peace.
          —Luke 1:78–79

When You Are Weary

Jesus said: Come unto me, all ye that labour and are heavy laden, and I will give you rest.

Take my yoke upon you, and learn of me; for I am weak and lowly in heart: and ye shall find rest unto your souls.

For my yoke is easy, and my burden is light.

—Matthew 11:28–30

Jesus said: Come ye yourselves apart into a desert place, and rest a while: for there were many coming and going, and they had no leisure so much as to eat.   —Mark 6:31

. . . the times of refreshing shall come from the presence of the Lord. . . .   —Acts 3:19

They that wait upon the Lord shall renew their strength; they shall mount up with wings as eagles; they shall run, and not be weary; and they shall walk, and not faint.

—Isaiah 40:31

When You Distrust Yourself

I can do all things through Christ which strengtheneth me.
—Philippians 4:13

Stir up the gift of God which is in thee. . . .
For God hath not given us the spirit of fear; but of power, and of love, and of a sound mind.
—II Timothy 1:6–7

Trust in the Lord with all thine heart; and lean not unto thine own understanding.
In all thy ways acknowledge him, and he shall direct thy paths.
—Proverbs 3:5–6

Jesus said: I am the true vine. . . .
Abide in me, and I in you. As the branch cannot bear fruit of itself, except it abide in the vine; no more can ye, except ye abide in me.
—John 15:1, 4

Be strong, all ye people of the land, saith the Lord, and
work: for I am with you, saith the Lord of hosts: . . .
My spirit remaineth among you: fear ye not.

—Haggai 2:4–5

When You Don't Know What to Do

If any of you lack wisdom, let him ask of God, that giveth to all men liberally, and upbraideth not; and it shall be given him.

But let him ask in faith, nothing wavering. For he that wavereth is like a wave of the sea driven with the wind and tossed.   —James 1:5–6

When You Feel Called to
Be a Witness for Christ

(And, like Moses, you are tempted to say: "O my Lord, I am not eloquent . . . I am slow of speech, and of a slow tongue.")

And the Lord said unto him, Who hath made man's mouth? or who maketh the dumb, or deaf, or the seeing, or the blind? have not I the Lord?

Now therefore go, and I will be with thy mouth and teach thee what thou shalt say.　　　　　—Exodus 4:11–12

Must I not take heed to speak that which the Lord hath put in my mouth?　　　　　—Numbers 23:12

Take ye no thought how or what thing ye shall answer, or what ye shall say:

For the Holy Ghost shall teach you in the same hour what ye ought to say.　　　　　—Luke 12:11–12

When Your Faith Is Shaken

Lord, I believe; help thou mine unbelief.   —Mark 9:24

If we believe not, yet he abideth faithful: he cannot deny himself.   —II Timothy 2:13

Search the scriptures [John 5:39]. Faith cometh by hearing, and hearing by the word of God.   —Romans 10:17

Continue thou in the things which thou hast learned and hast been assured of, knowing of whom thou hast learned them;

And that from a child thou hast known the holy scriptures, which are able to make thee wise unto salvation through faith which is in Christ Jesus.

All scripture is given by inspiration of God, and is profitable for doctrine, for reproof, for correction, for instruction in righteousness.   —II Timothy 3:14–16

Follow after righteousness, godliness, faith, love, patience, meekness.

Fight the good fight of faith, lay hold on eternal life.
—I Timothy 6:11–12

Now faith is the substance of things hoped for, the evidence of things not seen. . . .

Without faith it is impossible to please him; for he that cometh to God must believe that he is, and that he is a rewarder of them that diligently seek him.
—Hebrews 11:1, 6

Though he slay me, yet will I trust in him.   —Job 13:15

I am the Lord: I change not.   —Malachi 3:6

Although the fig tree shall not blossom, neither shall fruit be in the vines; the labour of the olive shall fail, and the fields shall yield no meat, the flock shall be cut off from the fold, and there shall be no herd in the stalls:

Yet I will rejoice in the Lord, I will joy in the God of my salvation.   —Habakkuk 3:17–18

Watch ye, stand fast in the faith, quit you like men, be strong.   —I Corinthians 16:13

Examine yourselves, whether ye be in the faith; prove your own selves. Know ye not your own selves, how that Jesus Christ is in you?   —II Corinthians 13:5

Ask, and it shall be given you; seek, and ye shall find; knock, and it shall be opened unto you:

For every one that asketh receiveth; and he that seeketh findeth; and to him that knocketh it shall be opened.
—Matthew 7:7–8

Conclusion

For Every Occasion and Experience of Your Life

To every thing there is a season, and a time to every purpose under the heaven:

A time to be born, and a time to die; a time to plant, and a time to pluck up that which is planted;

. . . a time to break down, and a time to build up;

A time to weep, and a time to laugh; a time to mourn, and a time to dance;

. . . a time to keep silence, and a time to speak.

—Ecclesiastes 3:1–7

Rejoice evermore.

Pray without ceasing.

In every thing give thanks: for this is the will of God in Christ Jesus concerning you. . . .

And the very God of peace sanctify you wholly; and I pray God your whole spirit and soul and body be preserved blameless unto the coming of our Lord Jesus Christ. Amen.

—I Thessalonians 5:16–18, 23

Suggestions for Continuing Study

Following are all the Scripture references included in this book. If your reading of *Hid in My Heart* has led you into further study of God's Word, this list may be helpful to you in several ways.

1. *Finding a particular passage.* It may be that you will recall reading a passage from one of the books in the Bible, and that you do not recall in what connection it was used. The list of references may help you locate it. (Except perhaps in the Psalms or Proverbs, where there are too many!)

2. *Marking your Bible.* This book has been written *not* as a substitute for the Bible, but rather, as an inducement for further study of the Bible itself. When you have read *Hid in My Heart* you may be interested in marking in your Bible the passages that have spoken to your heart. Some people keep a thin ruler in their Bible and underline verses they want to remember, or to be able to find readily. Some draw

a vertical line in the margin beside the passage. Still others affix in the margin a narrow strip of gummed silver tape.

3. *Using a Concordance.* A Concordance* is a necessity for anyone seriously interested in studying the Bible as a basic guide for daily living. After you have marked favorite passages, you may find it rewarding to find other related Scripture verses by looking up key words in the Concordance. You may have a special notebook in which to record your discoveries.

4. *Recording progress.* If you embark on a regular practice of memorizing, you may like to mark in the Index the references you have memorized. You will probably want to review from time to time all those you have learned to be sure that they are firmly planted in your mind and heart.

* Recommended: *Cruden's Concordance* (Grand Rapids, Mich.: Zondervan Publishing House); hard cover or paperback.

Index of
Scripture Quotations